Contents

KV-676-810

5 and 7 time

Everything's alright

Tim Rice and Andrew Lloyd Webber

Here is a song from the musical *Jesus Christ Superstar* by Tim Rice and Andrew Lloyd Webber with an unusual time signature of $\frac{5}{4}$. It creates a gentle rocking feeling which suits the words and the mood of the song.

Learn the song first as a class, then try the added parts to create a fuller texture. Note the interesting clash between G# and G in the last two bars. It really is not a misprint! Decide with your teacher how you will end the song.

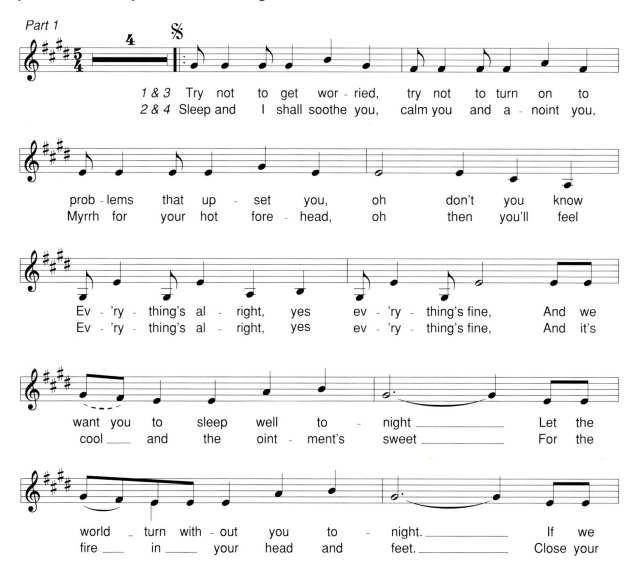

New Music Matters 11-14

3

Chris Hiscock and Marian Metcalfe

Heinemann Educational Publishers
Halley Court, Jordan Hill, Oxford OX2 8EJ
a division of Reed Educational & Professional Publishing Ltd

OXFORD MELBOURNE AUCKLAND
IBADAN JOHANNESBURG GABORONE
PORTSMOUTH NH (US) CHICAGO BLANTYRE

Heinemann is a registered trademark of Reed Educational & Professional Publishing Ltd

First published 2000

04 03 02 01 00
9 8 7 6 5 4 3 2 1

British Library Cataloguing in Publication Data
A catalogue record for this product is available from the British Library

ISBN 0 435 81092 8

Typeset and designed by Artistix, Thame, Oxon
Music typesetting by Halstan & Co., Amersham, Bucks
Picture research by Liz Eddison
Printed and bound in Spain by Mateu Cromo
Cover design by The Point

Acknowledgements

Grateful thanks are extended to Chris McGeever and the pupils of Hampden Park School, Eastbourne, to Lucy McKenna of Tanbridge House School, Horsham, and to the pupils of Seaford Head School for help with research and trialling, and to Clare Hiscock for general help, support and encouragement.

The publishers would like to thank the following for permission to reproduce copyright material:
Everything's alright, on pp. 4–5, music by Andrew Lloyd Webber, words by Tim Rice © Leeds Music Ltd 1970. Used by permission of Music Sales Ltd. All rights reserved. International copyright secured; *String quartet in F – 4th mvt.*, by Ravel, reproduced on p. 7 by permission of Editions Durand S.A./United Music Publishers Ltd.; *Take 5*, on p. 7, by James Cauty, William Drumond, Dave Brubeck and James Brown. Used by permission of Music Sales Ltd. All rights reserved. International copyright secured, Zoo Music and Warner/Chappell Music Limited, London W6 8BS. Reproduced by permission of International Music Publications Ltd.; *Mars, the bringer of war*, on p. 7, music by Holst, reproduced by permission of J. Curwen and Sons Ltd. Used by permission of Music Sales Ltd. All rights reserved. International copyright secured; *Diversion No.7*, by Richard Rodney Bennett, © Copyright 1965 by Universal Edition (London) Ltd, London. Reproduced by permission on p. 8; *Pentaseven*, by Marian Metcalfe, © Marian Metcalfe, used by permission of the composer on pp. 31–3, 34–5; *Old Joe has gone fishing* from *Peter Grimes, Op.33*, by Britten. © Copyright 1945 by Boosey & Hawkes Music Publishers Ltd. Reprinted by permission of Boosey & Hawkes Music Publishers Ltd on p. 13; *Piano Concerto No 2 in F, Op.102*, by Shostakovich. © Copyright 1957 by Boosey & Hawkes Music Publishers Ltd. Reprinted by permission of Boosey and Hawkes Music Publishers Ltd. on pp. 14–15; *Time Lapse*, on pp. 17–18, © Michael Nyman Ltd/Chester Music Limited. Used by permission of Music Sales Ltd. All rights reserved. International copyright secured; *C U when U get there*, on p. 24, words and music Ivey/Aldridge/Straughter/Straughter, © T-Boy Music, Boo Daddy Publishing Group, Du It All Music, Lek Ratt Music and Pooki Straughter Music, used by permission of IQ Music, Windswept Pacific Music Ltd (EMI Music Publishing) and Notting Hall Music (UK) Ltd; *Song for Athene*, on pp. 31, 32, by John Taverner. Reproduced by permission of Chester Music Limited.; *Twist in my sobriety*, pp. 40–4, words and music by Tinita Tikaram,

© 1988 Brogue Music, Warner/Chappell Music Limited, London W6 8BS. Reproduced by permission of International Music Publications Ltd.; *Ensemble Beethoven*, by Marian Metcalfe, © Marian Metcalfe, used by permission of the composer on pp. 49–51; *Façades*, on p. 53, by Phillip Glass. Reproduced by permission of Chester Music Limited on behalf of Dunvagen Music Publishers Inc.; *String quartet no 8 in C minor, Op.110*, by Shostakovich. © Copyright 1961 by Boosey & Hawkes Music Publishers Ltd. Reprinted by permission of Boosey & Hawkes Music Publishers Ltd. on pp. 54–5; *Siyahamba*, by Patrick Allen, © Patrick Allen, used by permission of the composer on p. 60; Country Boy Blues, on pp. 62–4, words and music by Richard Michael, © 1989, 2000 Stainer & Bell Ltd, London, England, from 'Small Band Jazz Book Three'.

The publishers would like to thank the following for permission to reproduce photographs:
p. 12 Redferns/Henrietta Butler; p. 13 Bridgeman Art Library/Rochdale Art Gallery, Lancashire UK; p. 16 Corbis/Underwood & Underwood; p. 19 The Kobal Collection; p. 21 Bridgeman Art Library/ Prado, Madrid, Spain; 25 (top left) Trip/F Good; 25 (top right) Bubbles/Lucy Tizard; 25 (middle left) Stone; 25 (middle right) Trip/A Bartel; 25 (bottom left) Corbis/Peter Turnley; 25 (bottom right) Tony Stone Images/Nicholas Devore; 33 Redferns/Mick Hutson; 34 Trip/Dinodia; 36 (top left, top middle, middle left and bottom row) SambaLa' Samba School of Long Beach, California/David Aguiar, www.sambacollection.com, www.sambala.org; 36 (middle, top right, middle right) Meg Sullivan; 37 Tony Stone Images/Ary Diesendruck; 44 Redferns/Carey Brandon; 45 Stomp/photographer: Junichi Takahashi; 46 Corbis/Archivo Iconografico S.A; 52 Corbis/Bettman; 53 Redferns /Ebet Roberts; 56 Mary Evans; 59 Redferns/Leon Morris; 61 Corbis/Bettman; 63 Redferns /David Redfern.

The publishers have made every effort to trace copyright holders. However, if any material has been incorrectly acknowledged, we would be pleased to correct this at the earliest opportunity.

The publishers would like to thank Gilly Marklew for the illustration on p. 45.

Tel: 01865 888058 www.heinemann.co.uk

Five beats in a bar

You are used to listening to music which has two, three or four beats in each bar. Before moving on you may wish to remind yourself of the feel of these times by listening to one or two favourite pieces using time signatures with 2, 3, 4 or 6 on the top line.

Now listen to four pieces which all have five beats in the bar. Try tapping the five beats lightly on your knee as you listen. Then jot down on paper any differences in the feel of the metre you notice between 5 time and the other times you have heard.

1   *Watching the aeroplanes* from *Fifo* by Francis Monkman (track 1)

2   *String quartet in F* (4th movement) by Maurice Ravel (track 2)

3   *Take 5* by Dave Brubeck (track 3)

4   *Mars, the Bringer of war* from *The planets* by Gustav Holst (track 4)

These four pieces all have a time signature of $\frac{5}{4}$ (five crotchets in a bar) or $\frac{5}{8}$ (five quavers in a bar). Five quavers are often written as a group of three followed by a group of two, but there is no reason why they should not be grouped otherwise or even all grouped together. Clap both examples below several times until you can perform them easily. Make the accented notes (>) louder:

a $\frac{5}{4}$ **time**

b $\frac{5}{8}$ **time**

Sometimes composers choose to use a repeated rhythmic pattern of notes, a riff or even an ostinato to underpin the rhythm and knit the piece together. Look at a repeated pattern of notes from each of the above pieces. Perform the patterns, repeating them several times, and then listen to each piece again concentrating on hearing the patterns throughout.

1   **Riff from *Watching the aeroplanes***

2   Pattern used by each instrument in turn and together in Ravel's *Quartet*

> When composers have a pair of semiquavers where each note of the pair is at the same pitch, they sometimes use an abbreviation ♪ . So, for example, bar 1 above is played:

3   Riff from *Take 5*

4   Ostinato from *Mars, the Bringer of war*

> **Discussion starters**
>
> In your groups and with your teacher, discuss any reasons you can think of why composers might choose to write a piece in 5 time, and any problems you think they might meet.
>
> What difficulties might you have in performing a piece in 5 time? Why should 5 time present problems in an otherwise metric age, where counting systems are based on tens?

Diversions no 7

Richard Rodney Bennett

Pentaseven

Marian Metcalfe

Another interesting time signature sometimes used by composers has seven beats in a bar. It is usually grouped as 2+2+3, but this is not always the case. Look at *Pentaseven* which follows the 2+2+3 grouping. The parts in this piece are graded in order, Part 1 being the most difficult. First clap the ostinato in Part 4 together to get used to this new rhythm. Then choose the right part for you and learn *Pentaseven* together as a class.

Old Joe has gone fishing

Opposite is a three-part round in $\frac{7}{4}$ time. It comes from the opera *Peter Grimes* by Benjamin Britten which was composed in 1945. The story of *Peter Grimes* is set in about 1830 in a fishing community on the Suffolk coast. Peter Grimes is a loner, a difficult and distrusted fisherman accused of causing the death of his young apprentice. Although he is cleared of the charge, the community remains suspicious of him. The round comes from Act 1, scene 2 which takes place in the village pub. Although it is past closing time, the pub is full of people sheltering from a violent storm. The coast road has been flooded and a landslide has swept away part of the cliff up by Grimes' hut. Anxiety for Peter Grimes' new apprentice raises tension and eventually someone starts a round to ease the atmosphere as they wait for news.

In the opera there are other layers of music going on at the same time as the story unfolds. Sing the round accompanied on the keyboard or piano to get the feel of $\frac{7}{4}$ time.

A scene from Benjamin Britten's opera *Peter Grimes*

Old Joe has gone fishing by Benjamin Britten

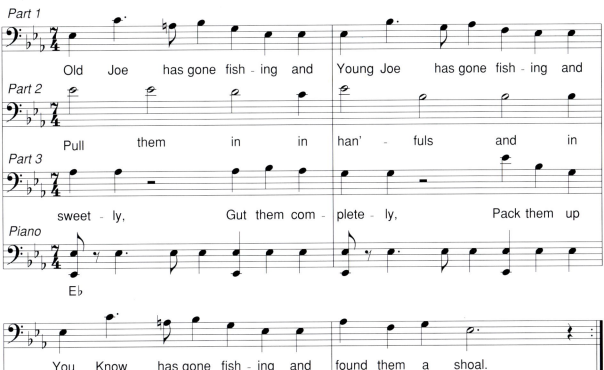

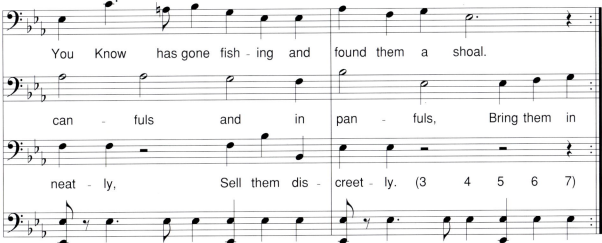

Now listen to this round in the opera as the composer intended it to be performed (track 7). You will hear several solo voices begin the round, singing each phrase twice before starting the next one. You will also hear one or two characters singing a phrase which includes a rising or descending scale to the words 'O haul away'. Follow your score as best you can while you listen.

Fishing boat about 1830

Listening to a piece which uses 7 time

Listen to the third movement of *Piano Concerto no 2* Op 102 by Shostakovich (track 8), first published in 1957. You may remember that a concerto is a substantial piece of music in which a solo instrument or a small group of solo instruments is set against a larger body of instruments or even a whole orchestra. This piece uses a standard classical symphony orchestra with the addition of a piccolo, two extra horns and a side drum.

Orchestra used	
Piccolo	Timpani (kettle drums)
2 Flutes	Violins 1 and 2
2 Oboes	Violas
2 Clarinets in B♭	Cellos
2 Bassoons	Double basses
4 Horns in F	Solo piano
Side drum	

The third movement is built on three main ideas, the second of which is in $\frac{7}{8}$. The use of $\frac{7}{8}$ is very exciting because the change of time signature gives the music the impression of skipping a beat and falling over itself with excitement. Because this movement goes at a very fast tempo, play through or listen to each idea several times to become familiar with them first. If there isn't time to play them all, at least play the second idea in $\frac{7}{8}$ to feel the exciting rhythm.

Idea A

Notice that this idea uses a rhythm ♩ ♪♪♪♪ which is sometimes contracted (squeezed up) to make it feel even more hurried. It should be easy to remember.

Idea B

Notice that Idea B is mostly in sixths (each pair of notes is *six letter-names apart*), so you will find it quite easy to play on the keyboard with one hand, or by using two beaters on a xylophone. This idea is in $\frac{7}{8}$ time so it is easy to pick out.

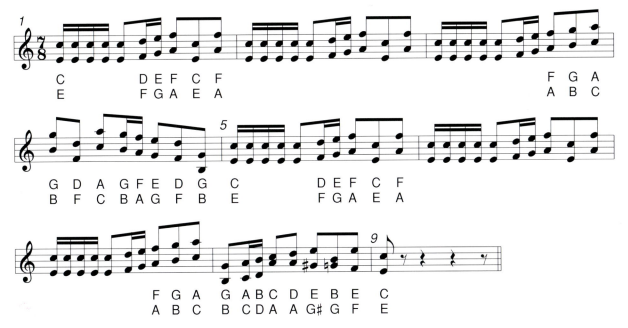

Idea C

This idea is also in parallel sixths (not shown here) and consists of running semiquavers. Notice also the changes of time signature.

Now listen to the whole movement and notice the way the composer uses the three ideas to build the piece.

Compare this movement with the rondo from the *Horn concerto* in E♭ by Mozart. Listen to the rondo following the chart in *New Music Matters 2* on p32 of the Pupil Book if it is available. Notice that here Mozart builds his piece by repeating the same idea or theme several times but separating the repeats with a number of different ideas called 'episodes'.

Shostakovich's concerto movement does not have the same structure as the rondo,

but is in what is known as **first movement form** even though it is not a first movement. In a first movement there are usually two main ideas called **subjects** which are introduced early on in the **exposition**. These are then developed in the **development** and brought back again in their original form in the **recapitulation**. This Shostakovich concerto movement has a third idea which is also introduced in the exposition, but the structure is otherwise clear.

Now listen to the Shostakovich again, following the structure on the chart on page 16 with your teacher.

Shostakovich: Piano concerto no 2 opus 102 – 3rd movement		
Bars 1 – 74	Exposition (This is an important section of a large piece where the main ideas are exposed for the first time.)	Idea A is played by the solo piano with a light accompaniment played at first by the clarinets and bassoons, then by the strings. The composer plays with this idea for a few bars and then …
Bars 75 – 108		… the time signature changes to $\frac{7}{8}$. Idea B comes in on the woodwind and horns while the cellos, basses and timpani mark the rhythm. Idea B is immediately repeated by the piano, with the strings accompanying to mark the rhythm. Here, too, the composer plays with this second idea before breaking out with …
Bars 109 – 132		… Idea C. This Idea reminds one of the type of finger exercises that pianists use to increase their finger dexterity (agility). Perhaps Shostakovich is having a joke at the pianist's expense. Whatever he is doing, this is a great chance for the pianist to show how fast they can play! The strings accompany this passage very lightly. Next comes the …
Bars 132 – 139		… codetta. A codetta is a short ending to a section – in this case, the exposition. It uses a motive from Idea A to lead into the …
Bars 140 – 284	Development	… development. In a development section new material is not normally introduced as all the ideas have been exposed during the exposition. The development section is exactly what it says: the ideas are developed. This means that the composer plays with his ideas to see what happens. Often he will take a small part of the idea and repeat it in sequence, or he will alter the intervals, or expand or contract the rhythm. He can do what he likes with his own ideas. In this development you will hear the three ideas being exploited in many ways, but you will be able to distinguish between them as the first idea usually maintains the rhythm, Idea B is always in $\frac{7}{8}$, and Idea C is the finger exercise.
Bars 285 – 336	Recapitulation (re = again; capo = the beginning)	In a recapitulation the main ideas are usually restated. In this piece, however, only Ideas B and C are restated during the recapitulation before heading into the final …
Bars 337 – end		coda – the ending. This is based on Idea A to round off the whole movement.

Introducing Dimitri Shostakovich

Dates: 1906–1975

Native country: Russia.

Musical background: He began the piano at nine, and also composed from an early age. His first symphony was performed when he was nineteen and was an instant success. More success followed as his output increased, and his music was played by conductors both in and outside Russia. Then Shostakovich fell foul of the Soviet leaders and his music was discredited. During his life Shostakovich's relationship with Stalin was crucial: Stalin inflicted severe trials and public humiliation on the composer, yet he also rewarded him with the highest titles and honour as his music was used in Soviet propaganda. He also received great acclaim from conductors and music lovers in Europe and America, but he died a deeply unhappy and isolated man.

What types of music did he write best? Symphonies.

Why is he remembered? He managed to write wonderful music whilst living in a difficult political and cultural climate.

Some of his other pieces: *Leningrad symphony, Twenty-four preludes and fugues,* string quartets and works for the cello.

Ground bass variations

Performing Time lapse

Michael Nyman

Time lapse by Michael Nyman was originally composed for a film called *A zed & two noughts,* produced in 1984. Most unusually, the director, Peter Greenaway, asked for a recording of the music to be given to him before filming began and then planned the scenes with the feeling and mood of the music in his mind. Because it was composed before filming took place, the music for *A zed & two noughts* works just as well without the film as with it.

Time lapse is composed using a **ground bass** and a repeating chord sequence. A ground bass is a sequence of bass notes that repeats throughout an entire piece. This device was used particularly frequently by composers of the baroque period (1600–1750). This period inspired Michael Nyman and many of his compositions reflect this baroque influence.

Learn the ground bass part together as a class, and then add the chord parts below and melodies on page 18.

Note: All the parts fit together and can be played at the same time.

Next allocate parts to individuals or groups and plan a class performance of the piece. You will need to:

- decide how many times the ground bass should be repeated, and on which repetitions the chord parts and melodies should enter
- decide how to start and end the class performance
- write down a plan of your class performance (who does what and when).

Ground bass variations

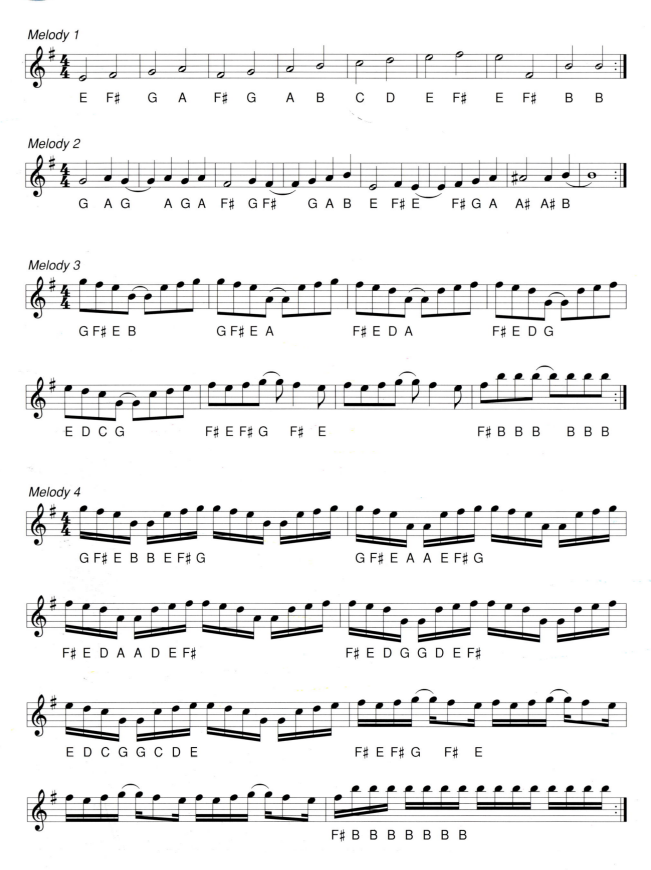

Listening to Time lapse

Listen to a performance of *Time lapse* by the Michael Nyman Band (track 9). This piece is in $\frac{4}{4}$ time and begins with an 8-bar introduction *before* the ground bass appears.

Note: You will need to count through this introduction to be ready for the ground bass.

Now answer the following questions:

1   After the 8-bar introduction, how many times is the ground bass heard? Make a list of the number of each repetition on the left of your page as you listen.

2   Write beside each numbered repetition:
   either **a**   chords alone plus ground bass
   or   **b**   the number(s) of the melody(s) from page 18 played with the ground bass

3   The chords are most often played as crotchet beats. In which repetition are some chord notes played as *semibreves?*

4   How successful, and why, do you think Michael Nyman has been in:
   a   holding the listener's attention throughout *Time lapse?*
   b   ending the piece?

   Give musical reasons for your answer.

5   The title of the film, *A zed & two noughts,* gives little indication of the story or images in the film. Imagine you are directing a scene to fit the mood of the piece *Time lapse.*
   a   What single quality or feeling would you take from the music and use as a starting point to direct a scene? Why?
   b   Describe in musical terms how this chosen quality or feeling is created in the music.

6   Name the instruments you can hear in this piece.

A scene from Peter Greenaway's film *A zed & two noughts*

Tension and relaxation – suspension

The chords in *Time lapse* are important in setting the character and mood of the piece. Some of the chords are triads whilst others contain four different notes. The chords in this sequence with four *different* notes have a much more 'tense' quality. Perform the chords and notice which sound tense and which sound relaxed.

Chord no.	1	2	3	4	5	6	7	8
Chord part 3	B	A	A	G	G	F#	F#	F#
Chord part 2	G	G	F#	F#	E	E	E	E – D#
Chord part 1	E	E	D	D	C	C	C#	B
Ground bass	E	C	D	B	C	A	A#	B

The intervals between notes of a chord decide whether a chord sounds tense or relaxed. Intervals of a 3rd between chord notes give a relaxed, blended sound. Intervals of a 2nd between chord notes often give a tense quality. In this example each 4-note chord contains the interval of a 2nd and this gives the chord a more tense feeling. Can you spot where the intervals of a 2nd are in each chord?

Perform Chord parts 2 and 3 *only* and notice how the alternation of relaxed 3rds and tense 2nds gives a strong feeling of movement and direction. This effect is created by the use of **suspensions**. A suspension occurs when a note of a chord continues to sound (is suspended) while a second chord is played.

Look more closely at the way in which suspensions work in Parts 2 and 3.

Chord no.	1	2	3	4	5	6	7	8
Chord part 3	B	A	A	G	G	F#	F#	F#
Chord part 2	G	G	F#	F#	E	E	E	E – D#

Chord no.	Note position	Quality of sound
1	B and G are a 3rd apart	relaxed
2	Part 3 moves to A, Part 2 stays on G – A and G are a 2nd apart	tense
3	Part 2 moves to F#, Part 3 stays on A – A and F# are a 3rd apart	relaxed
4	Part 3 moves to G, Part 2 stays on F# – G and F# are a 2nd apart	tense
5	Part 2 moves to E, Part 3 stays on G – E and G are a 3rd apart	relaxed
6	Part 3 moves to F#, Part 2 stays on E – F# and E are a 2nd apart	tense
7	In this chord both parts stay where they are on a 2nd while other parts move	tense
8	Part 2 stays on E for two beats and then moves to D#, Part 3 stays on F#	tense then relaxed

Perform Parts 2 and 3 again to embed the sound of suspensions firmly in your mind.

Stabat mater by Pergolesi (track 10)

Now listen to the entry of the voice parts in *Stabat mater* by Pergolesi (1710–1736). *Stabat mater* describes the grief of Mary as she watches her son, Jesus, dying on the cross. The heartbreak of Mary is achieved by a series of suspensions which add intensity to a simple rising melody. Sing or play the opening printed below before listening to the excerpt noticing the sound of the suspensions marked by an asterisk*. The words translate as 'The Mother stands grieving'.

Stabat mater: Jesus' mother, Mary, watching her son dying on the cross

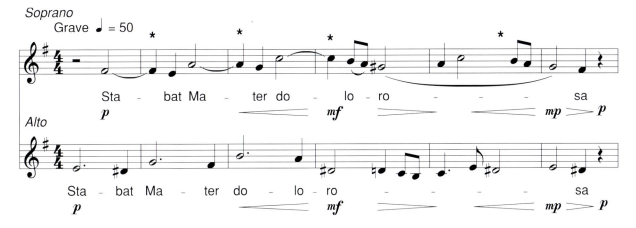

Listening to ground bass – old and new

Listen to excerpts from four pieces that use a ground bass. Two pieces are Baroque (written between 1600 and 1750) and two are from the twentieth century (written between 1980 and 1997). The four pieces are called:

Baroque		Twentieth century	
1	*Canon* by Pachelbel (track 11)	2	*The garden is becoming a robe room* by Michael Nyman (track 12)
3	*Here the deities approve* by Purcell (track 13)	4	*C U when U get there* by Coolio (track 14)

Listen to the four pieces and answer the questions below.

1 Identify which of the following ground bass themes is used in each piece.
Note: Only two of the three ground bass themes printed below are used. Each is used in one *baroque and* one *twentieth-century piece.*

2 Name the instrument or instruments that play the ground bass in each piece.

3 In your opinion, in what way does the *modernization* of the two baroque ground bass pieces:
a enhance the music?
b detract from the music?

Justify your answers with musical reasons.

Performing Pachelbel's Canon

Perform *Canon* by Pachelbel. Pachelbel's original piece consists of a ground bass which repeats many times. On each repetition a new melody is added and the texture of the piece becomes gradually thicker. Plan your own performance of the canon using the ground bass and melody parts provided below and on page 24.

Note: Melody Part 7 is by Coolio and is taken from his song *C U when U get there.* *This melody may be combined with the others or omitted. Alternatively, it could be the foundation of a contrasting section in the performance plan. The melody can be sung and/or played and is particularly effective with a rock beat.*

Canon by Pachelbel

(adapted CH)

Vocal chants

Chanting is the name given to an ancient style of singing that is most often associated with rituals and special occasions. It is common to every culture and chants are sung in all sorts of different contexts. In the British Isles, for example, chants are heard at football or rugby matches, in churches, mosques and temples, in school playgrounds and at political rallies. Chants are simple and uncluttered, and are usually sung in unison or with an easy backing. They generally have a clear message that is put across through easily remembered repetitive melodies.

Chanting in Britain today

Worshippers at a Hindu temple

Chanting in a school playground

Children chanting the Qur'an

Protesters lobbying

Chanting at a peace rally

Buddhist monks chanting Zen

Listening to chants

Listen to four chants from different parts of the world and answer the questions below. The four chants are called:

A *Resonemus hoc natali* from twelfth-century France (track 15)

B *Polegnala e pschenitza,* a harvest chant from Thrace, Bulgaria (track 16)

C *Yâ turâ ba 'd al bi'âdi* from Syria (track 17)

D *Geetaa* from India (track 18)

1 Match each chant with *one* statement or answer from *each* of the boxes below.

a

types of voice

i solo male
ii solo female
iii men's voices
iv solo female with
    women's voices
v solo male with
    men's voices

b

accompaniment features

i instruments play the vocal
   melody with some
   ornamentation
ii vocal drone
iii instrumental drone
iv oom-cha chords
v solo voice answered by
   a solo instrument with a
   drone throughout

c

structure

i AA
ii ‖:AAB:‖
iii AABC
iv AA coda
v ABCD

2 Match each vocal chant to *one* of the notated melodies below:

Performing a chant: Prabhujee

Ravi Shankar arr. CH

Prabhujee is an Indian chant composed by Ravi Shankar. Perform the chant in unison and then add backing vocal and instrumental parts. Instrumental parts are provided in the Teacher's Resource Pack (TRP 9,3,ia). A translation of the Sanskrit words is written below. 'Tantra' means Hindu or Buddhist religious writings and 'mantra' means a meditation chant.

> **Translation of *Prabhujee***
>
> Oh Master, show some compassion on me, please come and dwell in my heart.
> Because without you, it is painfully lonely, fill this empty pot with the nectar of love.
> I do not know any tantra, mantra or ritualistic worship, I know and believe only in you,
> I have been searching for you all over the world, please come and hold my hand now.

Perform the sections of the piece in the following order:

Either: **A B A C A Coda**
Or: **A B A Coda**

Section A

Section C

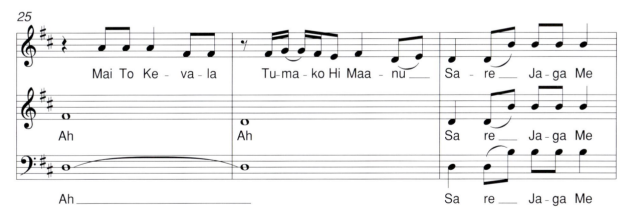

Ab - ba To Aak - ra ____ Baa-han Dha - ro ____ Ab - ba To Aak - ra ____

Ab - ba To Aak - ra ____ Baa-han Dha - ro ____ Ab - ba To Aak - ra ____

Ab - ba To Aak - ra ____ Baa-han Dha - ro ____ Ab - ba To Aak - ra ____

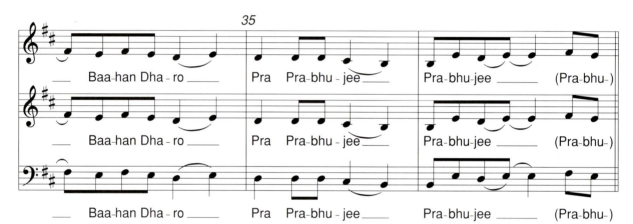

35

____ Baa-han Dha - ro ____ Pra Pra-bhu – jee ____ Pra-bhu-jee ____ (Pra-bhu-)

____ Baa-han Dha - ro ____ Pra Pra-bhu – jee ____ Pra-bhu-jee ____ (Pra-bhu-)

Baa-han Dha - ro ____ Pra Pra-bhu - jee ____ Pra-bhu-jee ____ (Pra-bhu-)

Coda

Part 1 *Repeat a number of times and fade*

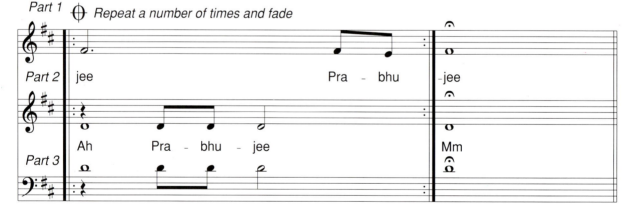

Part 2 jee Pra – bhu -jee

Ah Pra - bhu – jee Mm

Part 3

Ah Pra - bhu - jee Mm

Sing either Ah or words in Parts 2 and 3, Coda

In memoriam: Song for Athene

Throughout the ages chants have been used by a great number of western composers in their music. Because of their ancient associations with ritual and ceremony, composers have used existing chants or composed music that sounds like chants to create this particular effect in their music.

Listen to two pieces by John Taverner, both written in memory of people very close to him. Grief is a powerful and very personal emotion and some of the greatest works of art have been created in memory of a loved one. These two pieces are called *Song for Athene* and *Depart in peace.* Both are religious pieces that use chants to deliver their message.

Song for Athene by John Taverner

Song for Athene is a choral piece written by John Taverner in memory of Athene Hariades, a young family friend who was tragically killed in a cycling accident. The piece is well known because it was used at the end of Diana, Princess of Wales' funeral in 1997, in Westminster Abbey. The words of *Song for Athene* in the box above are taken from a combination of the Greek Orthodox liturgy and *Hamlet* by William Shakespeare.

1	*Alleluia* major
2	May flights of angels sing thee to thy rest.
3	*Alleluia* mi
4	Remember me, O Lord, when you come into your kingdom.
5	*Alleluia*
6	Give rest, O Lord, to your handmaid who has fallen asleep.
7	*Alleluia* major
8	The choir of saints have found the well-spring of life and door of paradise.
9	*Alleluia* major
10	Life: a shadow and a dream. minor
11	*Alleluia* minor
12	Weeping at the grave creates the song: Alleluia. minor
13	*Alleluia*
14	Come, enjoy rewards and crowns I have prepared for you.
15	*Alleluia*

Song for Athene is based on the following chant which is repeated a number of times in the piece. Perform the chant to familiarize yourself with it, and then listen to the excerpt which begins at **line 7.**

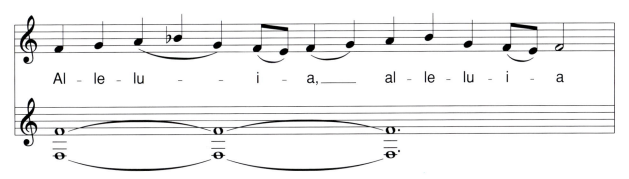

Al – le – lu – – i – a,___ al – le – lu – i – a

At different times during *Song for Athene,* notice that the texture of the music changes. These different textures are:

a   unison over a drone backing (as on the previous page)

b   parallel motion over the same drone backing, e.g:

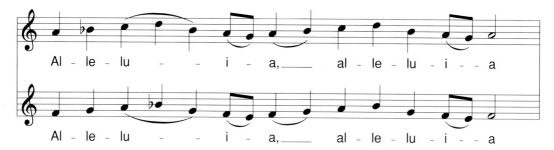

c   contrary motion where the lower part is an exact mirror image of the higher part, over the same drone backing:

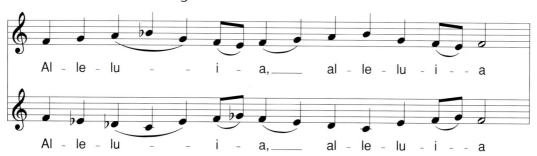

Listening to *Song for Athene*

Listen to *Song for Athene* (track 19) following the numbered lines of text printed on the previous page, starting at line 7. Before listening to the excerpt, list the numbered lines of text from 7–15 down the left-hand side of a page in your exercise book. Write your answers to the following questions next to these numbers.

1   For each setting of the word *alleluia* (odd numbered lines only), write down which of the following types of scale is used:
a   major
b   minor

2   For each of the even numbered lines only, write down the statement that matches the vocal texture of each line. Choose from:
a   unison over a drone backing
b   parallel motion over a drone backing
c   contrary motion over a drone backing

3   For each line write down the appropriate dynamic marking(s), choosing from:
a   *pp*
b   *mp*
c   *crescendo*
d   *ff*

4   a   Comment on the mood of the music up to and including line 14.
b   Write down two ways in which Taverner sets the music of line 14 quite differently from other lines in the piece.

5   For the funeral of Princess Diana, *Song for Athene* was performed at the end of the service, as her body was carried out of Westminster Abbey. Write down the qualities that you think make this piece appropriate for the ending of a funeral service.

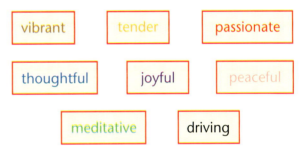
Listening to Depart in peace

Depart in peace was composed by John Taverner in 1998 in memory of his father. It is written for a solo voice, strings and tampura. The text is sung in Greek and tells the story of Simeon as an old man holding the baby Jesus in his arms and feeling that at last he can now die in peace. This story is interspersed with the word 'alleluia'.

Depart in peace consists of four distinct sections of music that are repeated in exactly the same sequence throughout the piece.

Listen to the separate sections (tracks 20–23) played in the *wrong* order (introduced on the CD as Sections A, B, C and D). Then answer the following questions:

1   Match *each* section with *two* statements chosen from:
   i   uses a drone accompaniment throughout
   ii   has slow moving string chords played at a low pitch
   iii   begins with a complete major scale ascending fast and descending slowly
   iv   has a solo vocal chant imitated by a solo instrument
   v   has strings played pizzicato
   vi   has a vocal melody with the following shape:

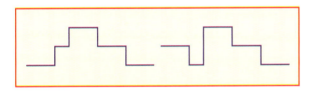

   vii   has three separated notes held on for a long time by a solo voice
   viii has rhythmic chanting.

2   From the list below, choose one word which describes the mood of each section:

   vibrant   tender   passionate

   thoughtful   joyful   peaceful

   meditative   driving

3   If *Depart in peace* were your own composition, in which order would you perform the four sections? Write down your answer and give a musical reason for each choice.

Next, listen to the whole excerpt (track 24) and answer the following:

4   Write down the order in which John Taverner uses the four sections.

5   Taverner uses an Indian scale and an Indian instrument in his piece.
   a   Why do you think he mixes western, Middle and Far Eastern sounds?
   b   In your opinion, how successful is this combination of sounds? Why?

6   Why do you think John Taverner uses chants in this piece?

John Taverner

Improvising using a non-western scale

During *Depart in peace,* John Taverner introduces melodies and textures that resemble the music of India. He achieves this by introducing the following features:

a   a non-western scale

b   a drone played on an Indian instrument called a tampura

c   an improvisatory vocal line echoed by a solo violin.

In groups of three, improvise a piece that uses some of the features found in *Depart in peace.*

Use the guidelines below to help you.

Player 1: Improvise an ostinato from the following notes and repeat it throughout. Start on the home note D:

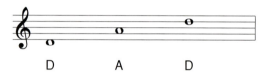

D   A   D

Player 2: Improvise *either* a vocal *or* an instrumental melody over the drone backing using the notes of John Taverner's scale:

D   Eb   F#   G   A   Bb   (or B)   C   D

- Begin and end on the home note.
- Move mainly in steps so that the shape can be easily copied by the second person improvising.
- If improvising vocally, bend the pitch of some notes up or down or decorate them with grace notes.
- Your improvisation can be made longer by adding other 'question and answer' phrases.

Player 3: Improvise either a vocal or an instrumental melody over the drone backing based on the same raga (see John Taverner's scale above). Your improvisation should echo as closely as possible the melody performed by player 2.

Indian street musicians

Samba Batucada

Percussion textures

Every culture in the world loves the excitement of percussion instruments. Whether accompanying songs, dances, rituals or ceremonies, they have presence and a direct physical impact. Apart from the human voice, percussion instruments are potentially the cheapest and most readily available instruments. Prehistoric man began the development of percussion using sticks, stones and bones, and since then, people have experimented and created these instruments from almost every substance and from a startling range of everyday objects.

Listening to music featuring percussion

Listen to four excerpts of music from different regions of the world and answer the questions below. The four pieces are called:

1 *L'Orient est rouge* from Serbia/Macedonia (track 25)
2 *Rag Jhinjhoti* from India (track 26)
3 *Mmenson* from Ghana (track 27)
4 *Element* from Japan (track 28)

Match each piece with *one* statement from each of the following boxes:

Beginnings/endings

a   the piece *begins* with a solo rhythm repeated four times before a second percussion instrument joins in with the same idea
b   the piece *ends* with an anvil, followed by a gong, and finally jingles
c   the piece *begins* with percussion playing this repeated graphic pattern:

d   the piece *begins* with a sitar improvisation accompanied by tabla

Use of instruments

e   this piece features a hand drum solo improvisation
f   in this piece individual percussion timbres can be heard very clearly
g   this piece is performed mainly by brass and percussion
h   this piece features the following riff pattern:

General features

i   the piece is played on percussion instruments only
j   this piece features the following graphic pattern played on wind instruments:

k   this piece has a drone note throughout
l   this piece begins with percussion instruments entering in the following order: high pitched bell – low pitched bell – shaker and castanet – high drums – low drums

Introducing samba

Samba is Mardi Gras or carnival music from Brazil that features a large percussion ensemble. It is music to dance to and has its own characteristic rhythms that distinguish it from other Latin American music. It originates in Rio de Janiero, the result of a unique musical fusion of Angolan African, Portugese and Spanish/Cuban cultures. Today different types of samba have evolved, but by far the loudest, and most brash, is Samba Batucada.

Samba Batacuda is a purely percussion form of samba and is very popular in Rio where a large number of samba schools exist. Competition between them is fierce, and each year the Mardi Gras celebrations include a huge street procession in which every samba school is represented, each competing for the prize of best performance of the year.

Samba is used as a backing to a song especially composed for the carnival on a theme such as the environment. The singers and the tuned percussion instruments ride on the decorated float and the percussionists walk, or rather dance, behind. Here in the UK, the style is catching on fast and most cities now have samba schools which regularly perform in carnival processions.

Listen to *Brasiliana* (track 29) which is a piece of Samba Batucada and imagine the excitement of the carnival.

The most commonly used instruments of the Samba Batucada

repinique

chocolo

apito

reco-reco

ago-go

surdo

tamborim

caixa de guerro

Percussion layers in Samba Batucada

The role of each of the percussion instruments in Samba Batucada is described in the box below.

Repinique This is a small high-pitched, double-headed drum used to play solo cues such as call and response patterns.
Chocolo This is a shaker that plays even notes throughout.
Reco-reco This is a scraper which plays the same time values as the chocolo.
Ago-go This is a cowbell with two pitches, one high and one low. The ago-go is held in the left hand and is hit with a drum stick held in the right. Notes can be dampened by the left hand to stop them ringing. Like the tamborim, the ago-go plays more complicated rhythms than the surdo or chocolo.
Apito This is a whistle used by the leader to signal an instruction to the group. Signals might indicate, for example:
   a   the start of a piece
   b   that the tamborim and ago-go change to a new rhythm
   c   a silent bar
   d   a solo improvised break, etc.
Tamborim This is small-headed drum with a single drum head. The player is able to press and tighten the skin or dampen the sound whilst playing. The tamborim is played with a single drum stick and plays more complicated rhythms than the surdo or chocolo.
Surdo This is a large bass drum which is hit with soft beaters. Surdos are the beat-keepers of the ensemble. They keep a steady pulse and alternate between higher and lower pitches. To achieve this, the surdo players are divided into two groups: high and low.
Caixa de guerro This is a snare drum which is played in the normal fashion of one hand facing upwards and the other in a loose closed hold facing downwards.

Listen to two excerpts of Samba Batucada:

1   *O Lodum* (track 30)

2   *Mistura 3* (track 31)

From their descriptions try to identify the instruments you hear in each excerpt.

Note: Not all of the instruments listed in the box feature in these excerpts.

Carnival in Rio de Janeiro, Brazil

Performing Samba Batucada

Below are four sections of a samba: Introduction, Section A, Section B and Section C. Learn each section separately. Perform each rhythm in each section before choosing a part that you feel comfortable performing. Play the *same* part in each section.

Memorize your part as quickly as possible. Samba rhythms are not normally written down but are passed on aurally.

Guidelines

1 Perform the Introduction and Section C together as a whole class.

2 Perform Sections A and B:
either   **a**   together as a whole class
or   **b**   in two independent groups.

3 Apito signals are given. These indicate the section that the leader wants to move on to in the following bar. These signals must be learned by everyone and should be clearly audible. You should respond quickly to each signal.

4 Between Sections A and B, a silent bar should be observed in order to make a clear break between them. This is shown on the score below.

5 During Section C, you will be directed by the leader to:
either   **a**   improvise a 2-, 4- or 8-bar rhythmic section individually or with others
or   **b**   perform as a group one of the parts from Section A (other parts may then be added gradually while some parts simply carry on with the previous section).

Note: Instruments can be easily made. Upturned plastic dustbins make good surdos. Tins filled with dried peas make excellent chocolos. Graters make excellent reco-recos, especially when scraped with a long toothed comb, etc. Different length iron pipes hit with a drum stick can sound similar to the ago-go. Old tambourines without the jingles or tambours can be used as tamborims along with any other finger drums.

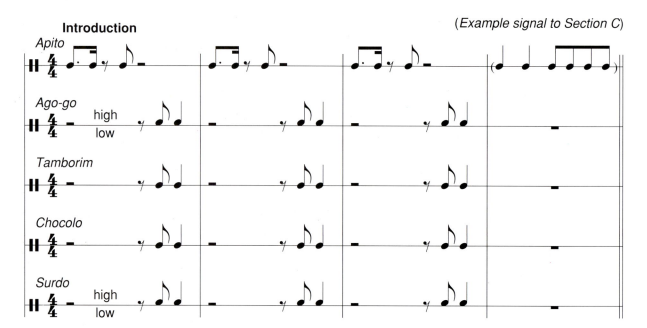

(*Signal to change to Section A*)

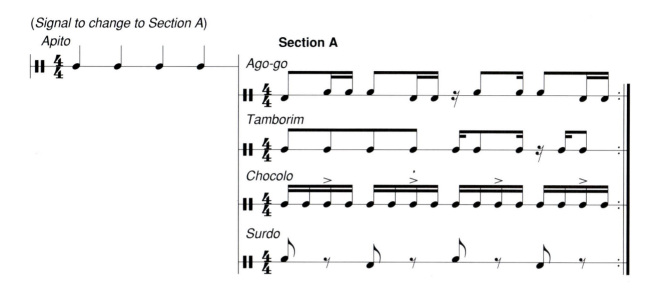

(*Signal for a silent bar followed by Section B*)

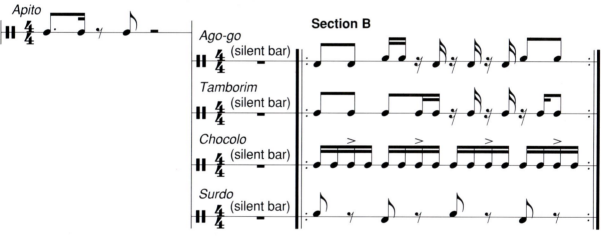

(*Signal to change to Section C*)

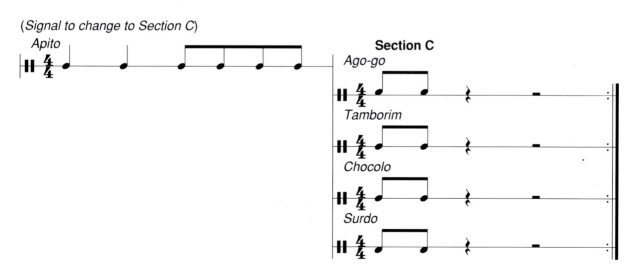

Project 4

Twist in my sobriety

Tanita Tikarum arr. Pet Shop Boys, adapted CH

Now that you have performed a number of different sections in the style of Samba Batucada, and know how to move from one section to the next, perform these same sections as an accompaniment to the song *Twist in my sobriety* by Tanita Tikarum.

Three groups of musicians are needed in the performance. These are:

1   vocalists

2   instrumentalists e.g. keyboard players

3   Samba Batucada players.

The vocal part is on this page and the next. Backing instrumental parts are included on pages 41–4 for a full arrangement of the song.

Keyboard voices are suggested for each part and when keyboards are played these voices should be used where possible. Balance the dynamics so that the percussion parts do not overpower the others. Use vocal microphones or keyboard amplifiers to boost the volume if necessary.

Finally, for the performance of *Twist in my sobriety* percussionists should perform each section in the following order:

> Introduction
> ‖: Section C   Section A   Section B :‖
> *(repeat x 3)*
> Coda *(continue playing Section B until signalled to stop)*

Part 8 (voice)

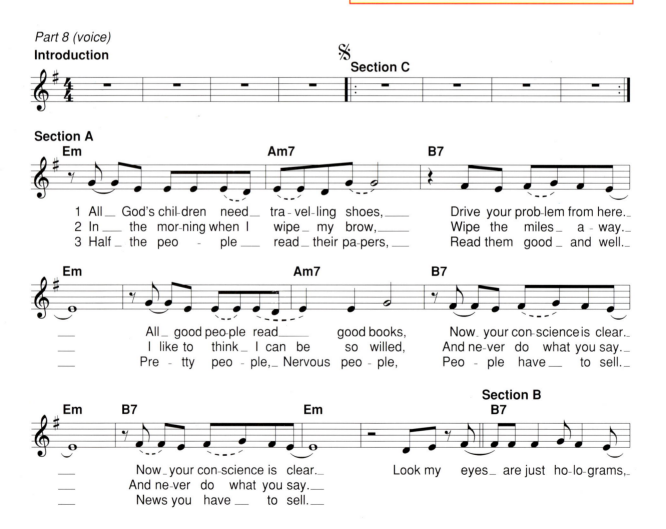

Em   **B7**   **Em**   **Am7**

_ Look your   love _ has drawn red from my   hands,   From my   hands   you know you'll ne-ver   be_

(To Coda on final chorus) ⊕   ⊕ **Coda**

Em   **B7**   **Em**   *DS*

_ More than   twist _ in my sob-ri - e - ty. _

Part 1 (trumpet voice)

Introduction   𝄋 **Section C**

    E

Section A

B   B   E A   B   E   G

Section B

B   A B   B

B   B C   C

(To Coda on final chorus)   ⊕   *DS*

B   A B   B

⊕ **Coda**

E

Samba Batucada

Part 4 (strings voice)

Introduction

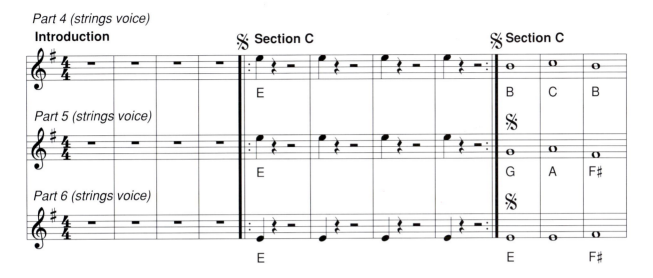

Part 5 (strings voice)

Part 6 (strings voice)

Section B

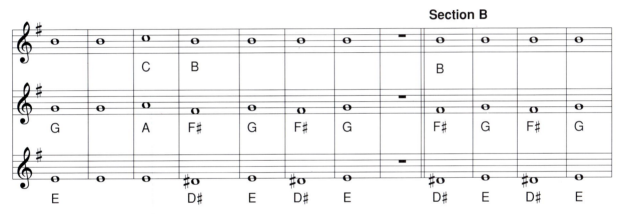

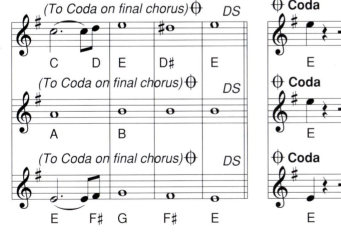

Part 7 (bass voice)

Introduction

𝄋 **Section C**

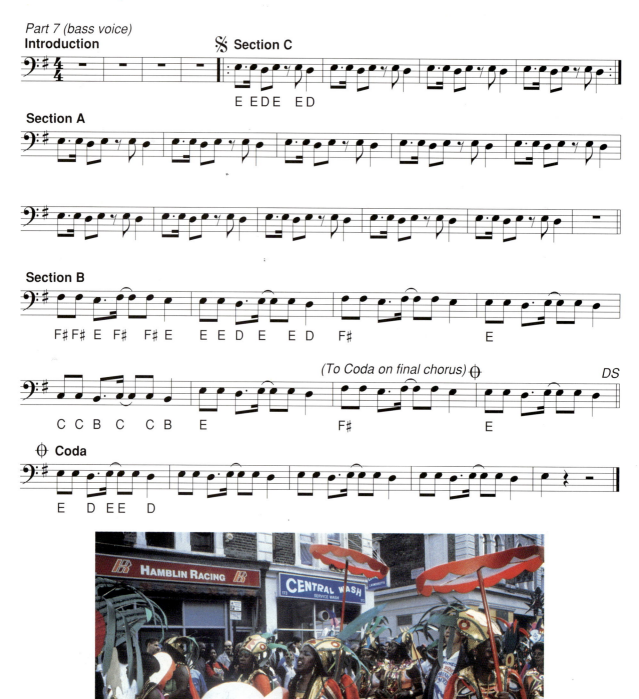

E EDE ED

Section A

Section B

F# F# E F#   F# E   E E D E   E D   F#   E

(To Coda on final chorus) ⊕   DS

C C B C   C B   E   F#   E

⊕ **Coda**

E   D E E   D

The Notting Hill carnival in London

Everyday objects – everyday music?

Many samba bands, particularly those from the poorer areas of Rio de Janeiro, use instruments made from everyday objects. Recently, the English dance group, Stomp, created an entire stage show accompanied by instruments made from everyday objects such as matchboxes, dustbins, cutlery and cooking utensils.

Listen to six excerpts of music (tracks 32–37) played on unconventional instruments and match them with the sound sources pictured below. Because the titles of the six excerpts give the answers away each is named after the performers instead:

Excerpt 1   The Baka tribe – Cameroon
Excerpts 2–5   Members of the group, Stomp
Excerpt 6   Students from the Karnataka
               College of percussion

The dance group, Stomp, using everyday objects to make music

Sound sources can be made from a variety of things

What is a motif?

Reading an orchestral score

Beethoven's fifth symphony is one of the most famous pieces of western European classical music in the world. Listen to the opening to remind you how it goes (track 38). Most people have heard this famous 'motto theme' at some stage of their lives and there are several well-known stories attached to it. Beethoven himself is quoted as having said of this opening, 'Thus Fate knocks at the door'. It was often played during World War II (1939–1945) because the opening motif of three short notes and a long note stood for the Morse code for the letter 'V' for Victory.

Now look at the first twenty-one bars of the whole score on pages 47–8. It has been slightly adapted to make it easier for you to read. You will see two sets of staves one above the other. Each set of staves is known as a **system**. You read along each system in order from left to right going from the top to the bottom of the page, as you would read a single stave of music or the page of a book.

Each bar (marked off by a vertical line drawn through the system) is also read vertically. For example, in bar 1 the clarinets, the first and second violins, violas, cellos and double basses all play their three Gs at the same time and follow that with E♭ played together in bar 2.

Now notice the clef at the beginning of the viola stave:

This is the alto or viola clef. When this clef is used it makes the middle line of the stave middle C so the notes on the alto clef read:

Ludwig van Beethoven 1770–1827

Beethoven has written ♩ = 108 at the top of his score. This means that, as there are two crotchets in every bar (= one minim), there will be 108 bars per minute or 216 beats per minute. This is extremely fast – probably too fast for you to follow the score at first. Listen to track 38 or perhaps your teacher can play these bars slowly on the piano while you practise your score reading. Start by following the first violins. Move your finger along the bars in time with the music. Once you can do this, try to follow both violin parts together, noticing the conversations they have as they pass the music back and forth between them. Then include more instruments, building up gradually as you become more skilled.

When you are ready, listen to the correct version and see if you can keep up with the music.

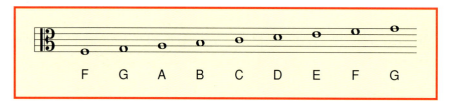

F   G   A   B   C   D   E   F   G

Symphony no 5 in C minor

Ludwig van Beethoven

Ensemble Beethoven

Marian Metcalfe

Practise your score-reading by performing *Ensemble Beethoven*. Each part is a different colour to make it easy to follow. At Section D, play either the notes with their stems down or the notes with their stems up (easier).

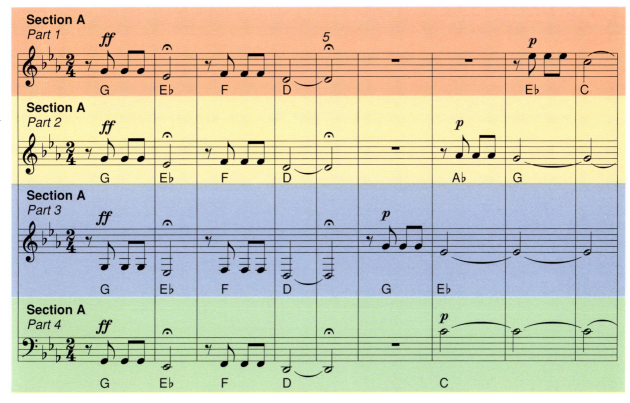

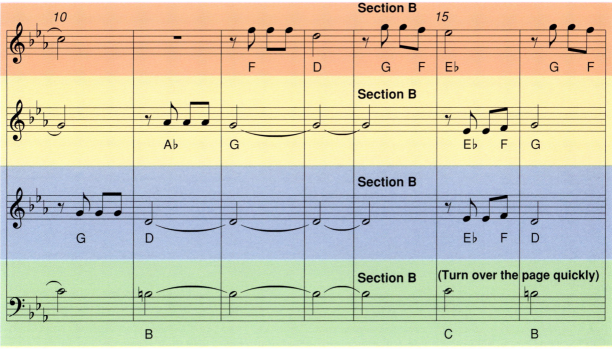

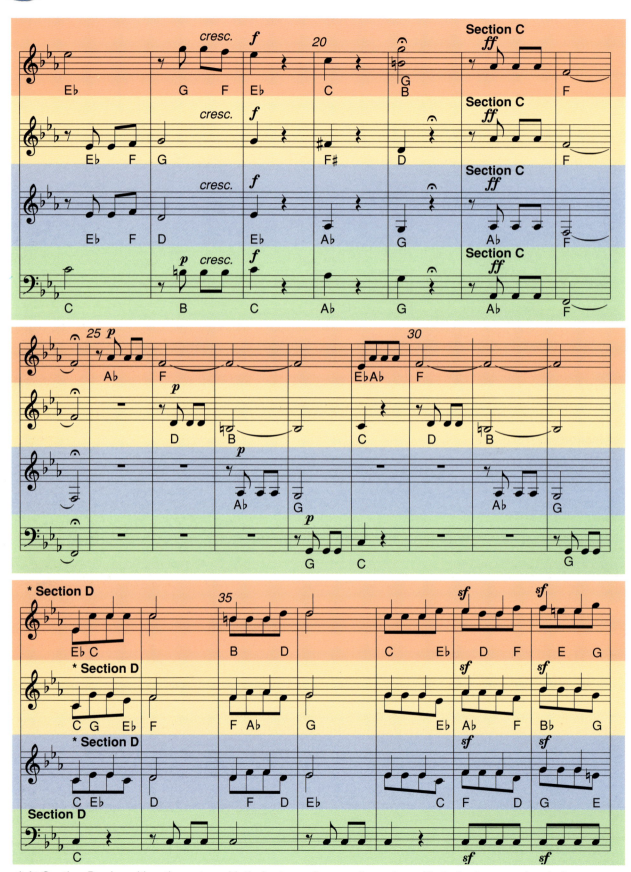

* At Section D, play either the notes with their stems down or the notes with their stems up (easier)

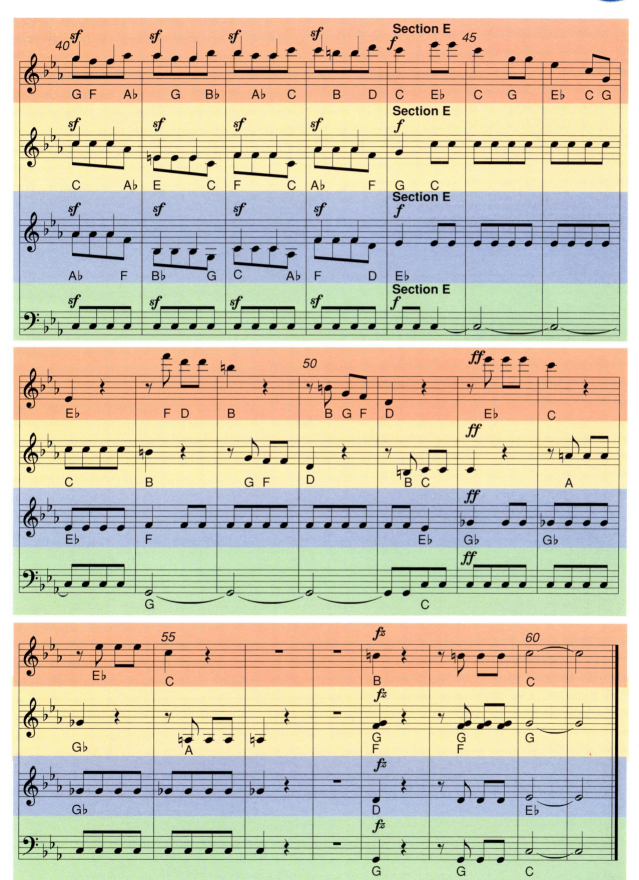

What is a motif?

In music, the term motif (or motive) is given to a short fragment or idea which has at least one characteristic which can be easily recognized, even when the idea is transformed in some way. One of the most famous motifs in music is at the beginning of Beethoven's *Symphony no 5*. It is used thirteen times in several different ways in the first twenty-one bars!

Beethoven conducting

This is the motif that Beethoven uses to build the first movement of this symphony.

Now notice how and where Beethoven uses it. It is not the same every time because sometimes the intervals alter, although the rhythm ♪♩ before the barline remains the same and the first two notes are always the same pitch. These two clues are enough to convince us that it is the same motif each time.

Now see if you can find the thirteen uses of the motif on the printed score on pp47–8. Write down the numbers of the bars in which it occurs.

Note: You are only allowed to count the motif once in any one bar!

Supposing this motif had been composed by you. Here are some of the possible changes you might have made to it without destroying it altogether.

Two quick-fire activities:

a Suggest four other changes that you might make to Beethoven's motif.

b Spot the changes Beethoven himself makes to his motif. Share them with the class.

Now listen to all of the first movement of *Symphony no 5* by Beethoven.

Listening to a minimalist piece

Façades by Philip Glass

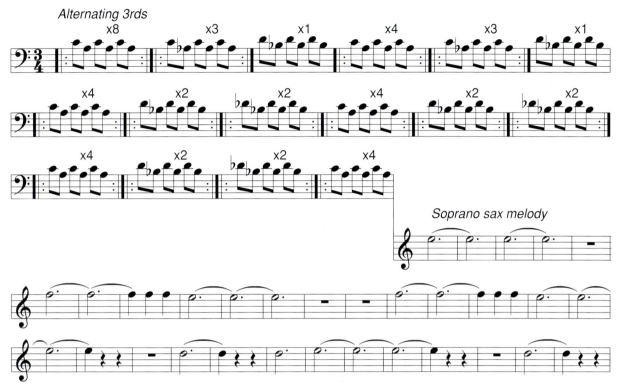

Listen to *Façades* by Philip Glass (track 39). Glass thought of *Façades* as 'theatre music' and wrote it for a film which consisted of images and music with no narration, principal actors or dialogue. This piece was composed with a picture of skyscrapers in Wall Street, New York, in mind, but was in fact cut and never used.

'Minimalism' is the term given to music in which timbre, density and rhythm are more important than melody and harmony. Ideas are deliberately limited to a few notes containing a small number of pitches and then these are very gradually transformed in tiny steps throughout a large number of repetitions. Repetition is the main structural principle, and minimalist music is notable for its constantly changing ostinatos.

Façades is a minimalist piece and is constructed very simply. It begins with an alternating minor third repeated twenty-four times. This is gradually changed, a note at a time, so the opening section of the piece, forty-eight bars in all, is built on these slowly changing alternating thirds.

After the first forty-eight bars, a soprano saxophone melody enters. This lasts for forty-four bars and is constructed from only four notes. This melody is then repeated twice, first with scalic decorations and then with a second soprano saxophone joining in. The alternating thirds continue throughout as a background.

Now listen to the first section of the piece, keeping one ear open for the alternating thirds throughout, and the other ear open to the way the melody moves away from the home note and back again.

Philip Glass at work

What is a motif?

Listening to pieces using motifs

Listen to excerpts from three twentieth-century pieces which are all, in their various ways, built on motifs. They are:

a The opening of *String quartet no 8* by Shostakovich (track 40)

b The opening of the 5th movement from *Turangalîla-symphonie* by Messiaen (track 41)

c *Eight lines* by Steve Reich (track 42)

The opening of Shostakovich's *String quartet no 8*

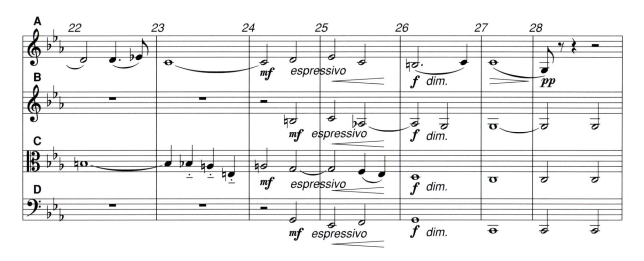

1   For the first excerpt the score is printed on the page opposite and above. Each bar is numbered, and the four instruments are, from the top stave down, first violin **A**, second violin **B**, viola **C**, cello **D**. Using bar numbers and the letters **A**, **B**, **C**, **D**, give the reference of each bar and stave where the main motif below begins. For example, the first time it is heard it begins at **D1**, i.e. in the first bar of the cello part.

2   For the second excerpt:
    a   listen carefully and select the correct rhythm for the opening motif:

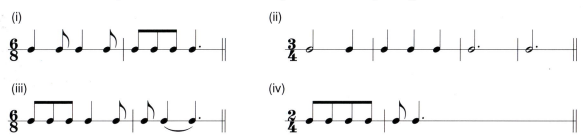

(i)   (ii)   (iii)   (iv)

    b   discuss the ways in which the composer provides variety in the music and keeps the interest going even though the motif is used so much.

3   It has been said of minimalist music that 'nothing happens and nothing is expressed'. Listen to the third excerpt carefully and then listen to the start of it again. Now compare the beginning of the excerpt with the end of the excerpt and discuss whether you think the remark that 'nothing happens and nothing is expressed' is justified or not, and why.

Gospel

Gospel roots

Gospel is a style of choral singing that grew out of spirituals. Spirituals combined African elements such as call and response and syncopation, with the harmonies and *a capella* style of nineteenth century hymns.

During the twentieth century, musicians developed the spiritual by introducing new elements such as blues, pop and rock. The resulting fusion, an exciting blend of old and new, is called gospel. Today the gospel style features in a great deal of commercial music, particularly pop, rock and jazz. However, in the southern states of America and in South Africa gospel is still a vibrant and popular ingredient of worship.

It is often the performers themselves who arrange their gospel performances.

Often they begin with a melody and then work out vocal harmony parts by ear, i.e. without the help of a keyboard or guitar. This is a skill that is learned through constant practice and experience. Once the harmony parts are added a leader then directs the performance, adding variety with changes of vocal texture, tempo, harmony, instrumentation and mood.

19th century worship in the southern states of America

Performing Noyana

1   To get a feel for the gospel style, perform *Noyana,* a traditional song of the Xhosa tribe in South Africa. Begin with the melody and perform it with the chords which are written above the staves. The words of *Noyana* translate as 'Will you go to heaven'.

2 Next add vocal harmony parts. These typically include:
   i   a part that moves in parallel 3rds with the melody (usually sung by tenor voices)
   ii a bass part using root notes from each chord (sung by bass voices)
   iii a fourth part that fills in missing harmonies (usually sung by alto voices).

3 Perform a three-part *a capella* version of *Noyana* (arrangement 1) which incorporates some of these features.

Note: Types of voices are not specified. Perform a part that is comfortable for your voice.

Noyana (arrangement 1)

Traditional Xhosa, adapted CH

4 Perform the second gospel arrangement of *Noyana* on page 58 for solo voice, vocal harmonies, piano and bass. Notice that in this arrangement:
   i   the melody is sung by a solo voice and is decorated in a blues style
   ii the vocal harmony parts are based on virtually the same chords but are arranged differently so as not to overpower the soloist
   iii the piano and bass parts add a slow rock feel.

Add a guitar and light drums if available.

Noyana (arrangement 2)

Traditional Xhosa, adapted CH

Listening to *Noyana*

Listen to *Noyana* performed by The South African Gospel Singers (track 43). The performance has three sections, structured A B A. Section A1 is not heard complete on the recording. Now do the following:

Compare Sections A and B. For each of the headings below, write down:

- any similarities between Sections A and B
- any changes that occur in Section B.

Headings

i dynamics   **ii** mood   **iii** tempo   **iv** metre   **v** instruments   **vi** solo voice/melody   **vii** backing singers/vocal harmonies

Harmonization

An important skill in gospel singing is harmonization. Harmonization is the word used to describe the process of fitting harmony parts with an existing melody. This means being able to feel which chords fit with a melody. For some, usually those who practise the skill frequently, harmonies can be worked out by ear. For others, chords can be worked out using the notes of a melody as a guide.

Gospel harmonies are often very simple and use mainly primary chords i.e. chords built on scale notes I, IV and V in any key. In addition chord V7 is frequently used, the 7th of the chord adding colour and making chord V move strongly to chord I.

It is possible to harmonize many melodies using primary chords alone. On the next page is the melody to *Siyahamba,* a traditional Zulu piece.

Gospel is a vibrant style of singing

Gospel

Siyahamba

Traditional Zulu arr. Patrick Allen

Siyahamba is in the key of F major. Primary chords in the key of F are:

The first part of the melody has already been harmonized and the chords are indicated in the boxes above the melody.

chord I = F   chord IV = B♭   chord V(7) = C

1   Perform the first section of the melody with the chords and notice how well the melody and chords sound together.

   The melody was harmonized by identifying the main notes of the melody, particularly those that fall on strong beats of the bar. These notes give clues as to which chord will fit:

- In the first two bars of *Siyahamba,* notes from chord I appear frequently and always on the strong beats 1 and 3 of each bar. These notes are shaded red.

- In the third bar, new notes appear on the strong beats of the bar and these match chord V. These notes are shaded blue.

- Bar 4 has one dotted minim F. This again matches chord I and is shaded red. However, the note F also appears in chord IV. Whenever a note is common to two different chords you must let your ear guide you. Perform two versions, one with chord I and one with chord IV. In this particular case chord I sounds more satisfactory.

2   Next perform the second section of the melody and work out which chords best harmonize each bar.

Note: Chord V7 is often used before chord I at the end of a phrase as it adds strength and makes the music sound more final.

3   As a class discuss which chords work best. Now perform the whole of *Siyahamba* with the chords.

Listening to gospel

Listen to four excerpts of gospel music. Three of the excerpts show the influence of jazz and rock. The fourth shows gospel used in the context of opera. The four excerpts are called:

> 1 *Matsheke Tsheke* arranged by S. Linda (track 44)
>
> 2 *Up above my head (I hear music in the air)* by Sister Rosetta Tharpe (track 45)
>
> 3 *The old ship* by Major Robertson, Daniel Towner and M. Cartwright (track 46)
>
> 4 *I'm on my way* from *Porgy* and *Bess* by George Gershwin (track 47)

1 **Matseke Tsheke**
   This excerpt divides into two sections of music. Each section begins with a solo female voice.

   a For each section comment on the use of voices and the vocal texture.

   b Which of the following describes the whole performance:
      i   unison
      ii   parallel 3rds
      iii riff
      iv   a *capella?*

2 Listen to excerpts 2 and 3. They are called **Up above my head (I hear music in the air)** and **The old ship.**

   a Compare the two excerpts, commenting on similarities and differences in:
      i   the use of voices and the vocal textures in each excerpt
      ii   the way in which instruments are used in each excerpt
      iii the way in which the mood and character of each excerpt is created.

   b Which features identify gospel in the two songs? Give reasons for your choice.

3 *I'm on my way*
   This excerpt is from the end of an opera called *Porgy and Bess* composed in 1934. Because it is set in the southern states of America, the composer deliberately copied the style of spirituals in his music.

   a Compare the following with *The old ship:*
      i   the solo singing
      ii   the choral singing.

   b Gershwin was influenced by blues and jazz. Which features of the accompaniment demonstrate this?

The American gospel singer, Mahalia Jackson

Performing Country boy blues

Country boy blues is an instrumental piece which mixes jazz, blues and gospel styles. It has four sections, an Introduction, Section A, Section B and a Coda. Perform them in the following order:

Intro (optional)   Section A   Section B   Section A   Coda (when indicated)

During Section B, improvise 4-, 8- or 16-bar solos using the scale below or the F major scale:

Country boy blues

Richard Michael, adapted CH

Introduction
Part 2 Freely in the style of a gospel chorale

A G   C F E   D Bb   C   A G   C A A   F F   E   A G   C F E

Section A Gospel rock ♩ = 80

D F   E   D   A G F A   B   Bb   A   E F G A   C A   G F

D   C   D D   F   F E

Section B

D   C#   D   A G F A   B   Bb   A   Bb   C   A   F G

F   E   F   D

Coda

F Bb   A   Bb   B Bb A   F

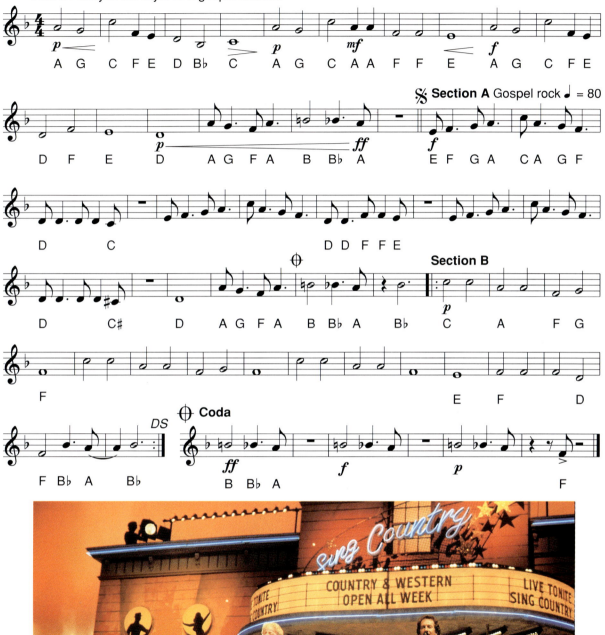

A country and western band

Introduction

Part 3 Freely in the style of a gospel chorale